A BODLEY HEAD NEW BIOLOGY

*Scientific Adviser: Dr Gwynne Vevers
Curator of the Aquarium and Invertebrates,
The Zoological Society of London*

HORSE, TAPIR & RHINOCEROS

UNIFORM WITH THIS BOOK

Bees & Wasps

Dr J. L. Cloudsley-Thompson, illustrated by Joyce Bee

Birds of Prey that hunt by day

Dr Clive Catchpole, illustrated by David Nockels

Chimpanzees

Prue Napier, illustrated by Douglas Bowness

Crocodiles & Alligators

Dr J. L. Cloudsley-Thompson, illustrated by Joyce Bee

Fishes

Dr Gwynne Vevers, illustrated by Alan Jessett

Frogs, Toads & Newts

Dr F. D. Ommanney, illustrated by Deborah Fulford
(Winner of the *Times Educational Supplement*
Junior Information Book Award, 1974)

Owls

Dr Clive Catchpole, illustrated by David Nockels

Spiders & Scorpions

Dr J. L. Cloudsley-Thompson, illustrated by Joyce Bee

Tortoises & Turtles

Dr J. L. Cloudsley-Thompson, illustrated by Joyce Bee

A BODLEY HEAD NEW BIOLOGY

Michael Brambell

Horse, Tapir & Rhinoceros

Illustrated by Douglas Bowness

THE BODLEY HEAD
London Sydney Toronto

Metric Conversion Table

1 centimetre = 0·39 inch
1 metre = 3·27 feet
1 kilometre = 0·62 mile

1 sq. centimetre = 0·15 sq. inch
1 sq. metre = 10·76 sq. feet
1 hectare = 2·47 acres
1 sq. kilometre = 0·39 sq. mile

1 kilogram = 2·21 lb (avoirdupois)
1 tonne = 0·98 (long) ton

Text © Michael Brambell 1976
Illustrations © Douglas Bowness 1976
ISBN 0 370 01593 2
Printed and bound in Great Britain for
The Bodley Head Ltd
9 Bow Street, London WC2E 7AL
by William Clowes & Sons Ltd, Beccles
First published 1976

Contents

1

Introduction

Horses, tapirs and rhinoceroses, like all animals, have to find enough food to keep alive; they have to keep out of danger's way; and they have to produce and rear enough young to stop their kind from dying out. These three sorts of animal, which look so different from each other and yet have so much in common, have solved the problems of living in three quite separate ways.

The horse has a stocky muscular body on long slender legs and a head supported by a distinct neck. Horses eat grass. They live on open plains and their feet are well suited for walking and running on firm flat ground. When danger threatens they run away, sometimes kicking out at the attacker before escaping. The foals, as baby horses are called, have legs almost as long as those of their mothers, so they are able to keep up with the rest of the herd when fleeing from danger.

The horse family, known as the Equidae, includes eight kinds or species of animals. These are the domestic Horse, Przewalski's Wild Horse, the Ass or Donkey, the Onager, the Kiang and the three species of zebra. Within some of these species there are several local varieties and breeds. The wild members of this family live only in Asia and Africa,

◁ Domestic Horse (shoulder height ranges from 0·8 to 1·8 m.)

but the domestic Horse and the Donkey have been taken to almost every place which man has colonized.

The tapir is a tubby animal with short legs, hardly any neck and an unusual snout which is rather like a tiny elephant trunk. Tapirs eat leaves of plants which grow in marshy places. Their feet are shaped so that they can support the animals in mud, where horses would easily get stuck. Tapirs are not fast enough to run away when danger is close. Instead they hide among bushes or in water with just their snouts showing above the surface. The coat of a tapir baby has a dark background, covered with lots of bright stripes and spots. With this camouflage the baby melts into the light and shade of the undergrowth and becomes almost invisible to an enemy.

Malayan Tapir
(shoulder height 1·0 m.)

White or Square-lipped Rhinoceros (shoulder height 1·8 m.)

The tapir family, the Tapiridae, contains four living species. They are found in South and Central America and in the south-east of Asia.

The rhinoceroses look very different animals from horses and tapirs. They are much larger and in some species their almost hairless skin is thickened into tough plates which protect them from the bites and claws of attacking animals. The great weight of the heavy barrel-shaped body of a rhinoceros is carried by its robust legs with wide feet. On the top of its nose there are either one or two horns, which stick out in front when the animal puts its head down and charges. Some rhinoceroses live in flat open plains and others in dense jungles. They eat leaves and grasses. Their feet carry them equally well on hard and soft ground, though rhinoceroses cannot run as far or as fast as horses. In jungle country they hide when they are threatened, but in the open spaces they cannot do this. They are too slow to run away so, instead, they turn to face their attackers and charge, tossing into the air any attacker they can catch. When their babies are born the mothers are more than a match for most animals that might attack them.

Rhinoceroses live in Africa, the south of Asia and in the East Indies. They belong to the family called the Rhinocerotidae and, of the five species alive today, two are almost extinct.

Horses, tapirs and rhinoceroses are not very alike, so why do zoologists put them together into one group? The reason is that all three families are descended from the same animals which lived over fifty million years ago. These ancestors were about the size of a terrier dog and they lived in forests, feeding on the leaves of low-growing plants. At this time there were many fierce animals which ate any plant-eating animals they could catch. Thus those plant feeders which by chance had slightly longer legs and so could run faster than their fellows were harder to catch and lived longer, leaving more descendants; and those which could run on the tips of their toes were faster than those which ran on the soles of their feet. Animals which walk and run on their toes are called ungulates; these include the horses, tapirs and rhinoceroses, as well as the pigs, hippopotamuses, camels, deer, giraffes, antelopes, cattle, sheep and goats.

Horses, tapirs and rhinoceroses are grouped together, separate from the other ungulates, because in them the third, middle, toe of the original five on each foot is the most developed. The feet are shaped symmetrically on either side of an imaginary line running down the middle of the third toe. This has resulted in these animals usually having either one toe or three toes on each foot, though in a few cases there are four toes on the front feet. Zoologists have called the group the Order Perissodactyla, meaning "odd number of fingers".

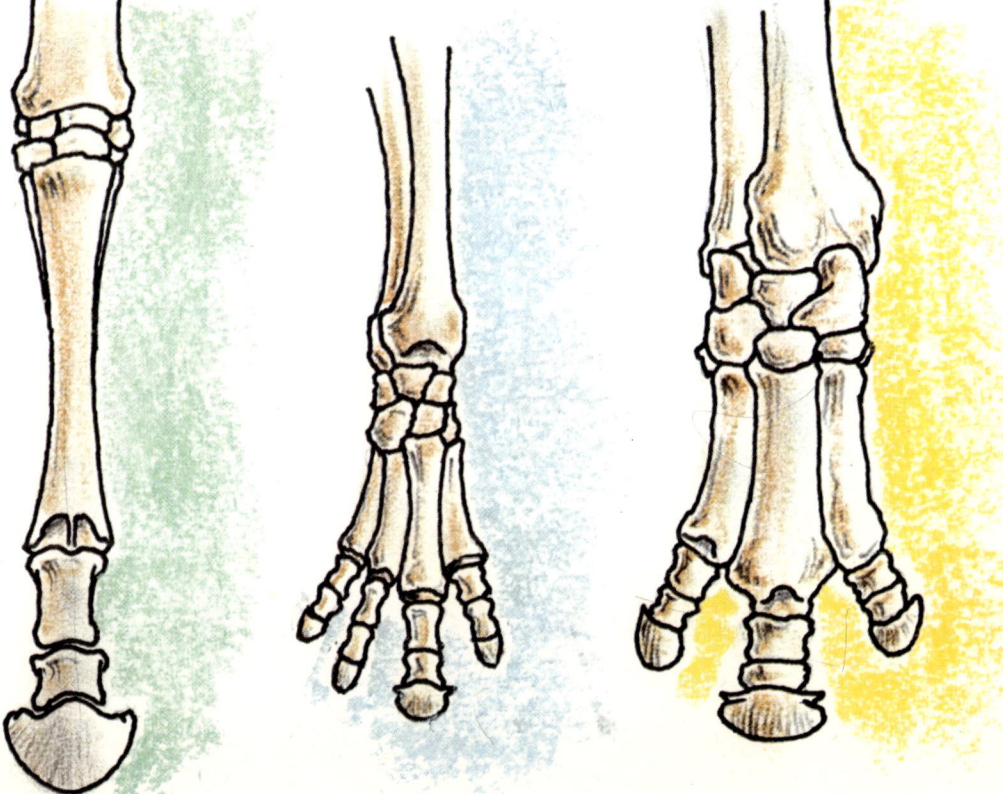

Horse   Tapir   Rhinoceros

The other true ungulates, the group which contains the pigs, hippopotamuses, camels, etc., have feet which are symmetrically shaped about an imaginary line between the third and fourth toes, so that they usually have either two or four toes on each foot and are known as the Order Artiodactyla—"even number of fingers"—though they are also often called the cloven-hoofed animals.

So for the last fifty million years the group of odd-toed ungulates, the Perissodactyla, has been evolving in competition with all the other animals searching for the first bite of grass. About twenty million years ago there lived eight other families of the Perissodactyla as well as the three that are alive today. Indeed it was only two million years ago that the last of these extinct families died out. At present there are only seventeen species of the Perissodactyla still alive.

2

Horses, asses and zebras

The horses, asses and zebras seem very much alike apart from the colour pattern of their coats. The head has a long strong blunt nose with a very deep jaw. The eyes and ears are alert, facing very much to the front. The neck is muscular and distinct, often with a mane of upright hairs forming a ridge from the top of the head to the shoulders. The body is barrel-shaped. The forelegs are long and straight. The hind legs are less straight and are very much more muscular, especially over the haunches, for here are the massive muscles which provide power when the animal is running. Each limb ends in a single horn-covered hoof.

The most obvious differences between the eight species are in the pattern of the coat though there is a great range of colours in the domestic Horse as a result of selection by man. The domestic Horse is descended from the Tarpans of western Asia and eastern Europe which only died out in the wild about a hundred years ago. Tarpans were about 1·2 metres high at the shoulder with a stiff mane and a little forelock, the hair which in the domestic Horse falls forward from the top of the head. The mane and the tail were dark and there were dark stripes on the back of the forelegs in at least some Tarpans.

13

◁ Tarpan

Przewalski's Wild Horses (shoulder height 1·1 m.)

The colour of the rest of the coat was grey to brown, probably varying with the district from which they came.

Przewalski's (pronounced Prish-voll-ski) Horse from eastern Asia is a truly wild animal. It was first described by the Russian army officer and explorer, Colonel Przewalski, about one hundred years ago. Perhaps a little bit smaller than the Tarpan, it stands at 1·1 metres at the shoulder. (It is much easier to measure accurately the height at the shoulder than at the top of the head because if the horse is looking upwards or downwards or just shaking its head the top is never in the same place for more than a few moments.) Przewalski's Horse has a stiff black mane and a white muzzle, the rest of the coat being a strong yellow-brown. It is now very rare if not extinct in the wild but is breeding with some success

14

Domestic Donkey (shoulder height 1·1 m.) ▷

in captivity, and for the time being has been saved from extinction.

Though the asses and the onagers are very like the horses, they are much closer to each other than to any of the horses or zebras. The Ass lives in the north-east part of Africa. The species includes two wild varieties, the Nubian Wild Ass and the Somali Wild Ass, as well as the domestic Donkey. Donkeys have a dark brown band running along the back, with a stripe across the shoulders, so that from above the marking appears as a cross. It is a Christian legend that donkeys have this mark in memory of the donkey which carried Jesus into Jerusalem.

Onager (often called Asian Wild Ass, shoulder height 1·0 to 1·3 m.)

The asses have much smaller hoofs than the horses or zebras. Living in rocky places where they have no need to spread their weight on the hard ground, they can get a safer foothold if the hoofs can be placed between loose stones instead of on top of them. Asses are noted for their long ears and for their harsh hee-haw bray.

The Onager lives in south-western and central Asia. Once the species extended without a break from Palestine to north-west India and to Mongolia, but as man has colonized this land it has become isolated into several local varieties.

In the great Central Asian plateau, in the Gobi

Grevy's Zebra (shoulder height 1·5 m.) ▷

desert, lives the Kiang. It is larger and more horse-like than the onagers.

The zebras may be descended from true horses or from wild asses. Certainly they look more like striped horses than striped asses, but this might be because, like the wild horses, most zebras live on flat grasslands. Indeed the most ass-like of the zebras, the Mountain Zebra, lives in rocky places.

There are three species of zebra. The north-east of Africa is the home of Grevy's Zebra, named after a President of France. This is the largest zebra. It has many narrow stripes and has a characteristic pattern on the rump.

Common Zebras live throughout the grasslands of east and southern Africa. Nowadays they are

split into two main groups: Grant's Zebra in East Africa and Chapman's Zebra in Rhodesia, Zambia and South West Africa. Chapman's Zebras have "shadow" stripes between the main stripes on the flanks, but these are almost totally absent from Grant's Zebras.

The third species of zebra is the Mountain Zebra, which lives in hill country in the southern parts of Africa and has much smaller feet than the other two species. This allows it to walk on the rocky and stony surfaces of the hillsides much more surely than if its feet were larger. It does not need to walk great distances over ground which can become very soft and where large feet are an advantage. Mountain Zebras have a "dewlap" halfway down the underside of the neck, and there is a very distinctive "gridiron" pattern of stripes at the base of the tail.

Common Zebras (shoulder height 1·4 m.)

Zebras live in herds, which may be very large in the wide open grasslands of East Africa where they are often found associating with even larger herds of wildebeest (gnus). In areas where there is less food the herds are smaller and the Mountain Zebras live in troops of only twenty or so animals.

The animals in the horse family are grazers, though quite often they do eat leaves of bushes and shrubs. They crop the grass with their strong front teeth and lips and chew it with their cheek teeth. Grass is abrasive and indigestible, but the horse's teeth are long and can last a lifetime of grinding. A horse cannot digest grass on its own. What it does is provide a home within its intestine for tiny organisms which break down the grass into material the horse can then absorb.

Females in the horse family are able to breed by the time they are two years old, although they go on growing for a few more years. Males can breed when they are about two and a half. Every third week the female "comes into heat" when she will accept the male. At this time she produces an egg which passes into her womb. The male becomes more and more interested in her, nuzzling and nibbling her until finally she stands still and he is able to jump on to her so that his chest is resting on the female's back and his hind legs are standing on the ground just behind her. This makes it possible for him to push his penis into her vagina and deposit his sperms at the entrance to her womb into which they can pass quickly. The female's egg is then fertilized by one of these sperms to form an embryo.

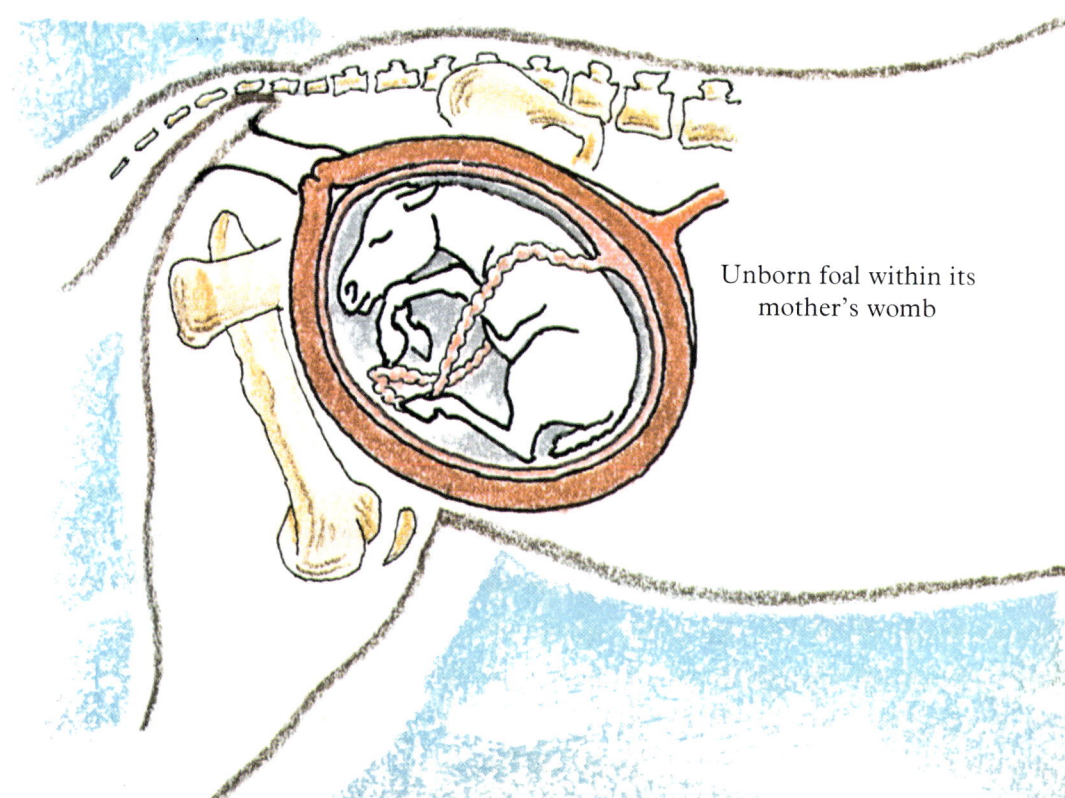

Unborn foal within its mother's womb

Young foal

Inside the womb the embryo begins to grow and as it gets bigger it becomes more and more like a foal. It lies curled up inside a protective bag and takes its nourishment and gets rid of its waste through the placenta, a special organ which only appears while the mother is carrying an unborn foal. In the placenta the blood of the foal and the blood of the mother are separated by a very thin layer of cells and the nourishment and waste can easily pass from one to the other.

In horses the foals are born usually about eleven months after mating; in zebras almost a year, and in donkeys nearly thirteen months. As soon as the foal is born the mother licks it dry and in a very few minutes it is able to get to its feet. The foal feeds by sucking milk from its mother's udder. When it is a few weeks old it starts to eat grass and by about 6 months has stopped sucking milk.

Horses move by walking, trotting, cantering and galloping. In walking and trotting only two legs are are off the ground at once. When cantering the horse skips with both pairs of legs. The gallop, which is fastest of all, is a series of jumps with the back legs acting together and with one of the front legs usually coming to the ground a little ahead of the other.

A horse may live for twenty-five years or more.

Horse trotting

3

Domestication

Horses, donkeys and mules are domesticated animals. They are used by man in his daily life and work. The Assyrians used the onagers to pull their chariots, and zebras have been used to pull coaches in the last century.

Horses were first domesticated in western Asia and eastern Europe perhaps about five thousand years ago and truly wild horses were possibly still being caught for this purpose until a few hundred years ago. The difference between domestication and taming is that domesticated animals breed regularly and do not need to be replaced by catching more wild animals. Once the animals are breeding when under man's control he can select which animals to breed from and so produce strains of fast horses, or strong horses, or nimble horses.

The donkey is widely used in poor areas. It eats less food than a horse so it is cheaper for the peasant to keep. Donkeys are sure-footed and do well in rocky country, and they can carry heavy weights on their backs.

The mule, the offspring of a mare (female horse) and a jackass (male donkey), combines the larger size of the horse with the toughness of the donkey. The opposite cross, the hinny, the offspring of a

jenny (female donkey) and a stallion (male horse), is much less useful and not very common. Mules are very strong and patient, but they also earn their reputation for being stubborn. They are quite healthy and live a long time but they are sterile, unable to reproduce with each other or with horses or donkeys.

Before a horse can be used as a domestic animal it has to be "broken in". This sounds much worse than it is. What is really happening is not breaking the animal's will to be free but making it so familiar with the ways of men that it no longer feels the need to run away whenever it is handled. A horse of any age can be broken in but it is much easier to break in a young animal.

At first the person breaking in the horse gets it used to taking food from his hand, then to having its head and neck touched, then to having a rope over its neck. After that a bridle is put on and the animal is allowed to exercise by running on the end of a rope. Later it has all its harness put on and finally, if it is being broken for riding, somebody gets into the saddle while somebody else holds its head. After this the horse and rider practise on their own. If it is to be used as a cart horse it must get accustomed to the feel of shafts and often a special, long pair of shafts without a cart is used until the horse becomes so familiar with them that it will stand still when a proper cart is being hitched. The whole process is

◁ Onagers: chariot-drawers of the past

Schooling a domestic Horse

one of practice with kindness and patience.

Harnesses have been made all over the world
and many different patterns have developed. The
most important part of a harness is the head harness
which often includes a metal bar, a bit, which goes
into the horse's mouth and which is attached to the
reins, the straps used to control the horse. A horse is
much more sensitive to pressure being applied to
the reins when there is a bit than when the reins are
attached direct to the head harness. Though a
horseman may ride bareback he is much more
comfortable when sitting in a saddle held on to the
horse by a girth strap under the belly. Stirrups in

which the rider can place his feet help him to ease his weight on the horse's back.

Cart horses have to have some way of transmitting the thrust from their legs through their bodies to the cart. They have a body harness to help them do this, which often includes a collar. The horse can push against this without throttling itself.

Draught animals which carry heavy loads on their backs have the simplest harness of all, usually two bags or baskets called panniers hanging either side and joined together by a broad leather band lying over the back.

Most working horses have to walk or run over hard road surfaces which wear away the hoofs faster than the horn can grow. To prevent this, iron strips (horse-shoes) are nailed on to the soles of the feet.

The things horses pull for man range from the trunks of newly felled trees through ploughs, tumbrils (two-wheeled carts), wagons (four-wheeled carts), barges and guns, to the beautifully decorated coaches of state occasions.

Working horses

4

Tapirs

Tapirs live in marshlands. They have barrel-shaped bodies which merge almost imperceptibly into the neck and the head. Their noses end in a long flexible snout. The back of the animal ends much more abruptly in a round rump with a short tail. The legs are short.

There are four species of tapirs. The largest and perhaps best known is the Malayan Tapir which lives in the jungle swamps of south-east Asia and Sumatra. The adults are black and white. The young are brown with white stripes running along the body.

The other three species live in South and Central America. The most common is the Brazilian Tapir. It is dark brown all over, and has a short dark brown mane extending the whole length of the neck. Its young is also brown with white stripes running along the length of the body; between these stripes are rows of fainter white dots. This tapir lives in the forest swamps of the Amazon and Orinoco basins of north-eastern South America.

Further to the west and living high up in forests on the slopes of the Andes is the smallest of the tapirs, the Mountain or Woolly Tapir. It has been found as high as 4,250 metres and it sometimes moves to above the tree line. It is mostly brown and its coat is thick and long to give plenty of insulation against the low temperatures that occur on high mountains.

In the north-west of South America and in neighbouring Central America lives Baird's Tapir. This is dark brown on the upper parts of the head, body and limbs but the side of the head and its underparts are much lighter and it does not have such an obvious mane as the Brazilian Tapir. Baird's Tapir is found up to 1,800 metres living in swampy rain forests.

Malayan Tapir (shoulder height of adult 1·0 m.)

Brazilian Tapir (shoulder height 0·9 m.)

Tapirs move by walking, though occasionally they break into a faster running trot. When they walk they tend to pick their feet up in a very deliberate manner, as if their feet are sore. This helps them make their way through the tough stalks of water plants without getting tangled.

Tapirs have often been thought to be wholly vegetarian, living on the soft plants which grow in wet places, but they also eat a lot of small animals which abound in tropical marshes. Much of their food is just below the surface so the tapir has sometimes to put its nose under water in order to eat. Maybe the flexible snout helps the tapir by allowing it to feed and breathe at the same time.

Mountain or Woolly Tapir (shoulder height 0·7 m.)

Baird's Tapir (shoulder height 1·0 m.)

Tapirs usually have only one baby, born after a thirteen-month pregnancy. The baby is suckled for up to six months by which time the coat pattern has changed. It is fully grown by four years and may live for thirty years.

5

Rhinoceroses

There are five species of rhinoceros alive today, although two are very close to extinction and none of the other three are wholly safe. Rhinoceroses are large, heavily-built animals which live on plant foods. Their most obvious feature is the possession of horns on the top of the nose in front of the eyes. The head is large, much larger than is needed to enclose the brain. It is used, with the horns pointing forward, as a battering ram. Not many animals can withstand being hit by the horns of a two-tonne rhinoceros charging at 40 kilometres an hour.

It is this ability to attack predatory animals coupled with having a thick hide, through which even a lion or a tiger has difficulty in biting, that provides the rhinoceros with its defence from perpetual attack. Other plant-eating animals rely on their speed to escape from predators.

Three kinds of rhinoceros live in Asia. The Indian Rhinoceros, which lives in Northern India and Burma, and the closely-related Javan Rhinoceros, which lives, or once lived, in Java, Sumatra and Burma, have only one horn on the snout. The third species living in Asia as well as in Sumatra and Borneo is the two-horned Sumatran Rhinoceros.

The Indian Rhinoceros is perhaps the most spectacular. It may weigh 2½ tonnes. Its body is covered by thick plates of pinkish brown skin which are separated from each other by deep folds of soft skin, allowing them to move when the animal walks and runs. Dotted over these plates are many small round lumps, all more or less the same size, looking like

Indian Rhinoceros (shoulder height 2·0 m.)

Black Rhinoceros (shoulder height 1·4 m.)

rivet heads. The Javan Rhinoceros is very similar in appearance, but is a little smaller and can be told apart from the Indian Rhinoceros by the shape of the shoulder plate.

The Sumatran Rhinoceros which has two horns is a much smaller animal. It weighs about one tonne. It has grey-black skin with a sparse covering of red-black hair, which gets thinner as the animal gets older. It lives in dense forests near to streams where it wallows in deep mud, and it feeds by browsing on the forest plants.

Two other species, both with two horns, live in Africa. The Black Rhinoceros, which weighs up to 3 tonnes, is almost hairless with dark grey-brown skin and lives in bush country. It is a browser. Its pointed upper lip grips twigs of trees and bushes while its tongue removes the leaves. Browsing rhinoceroses are usually found on their own except when a female is with a young calf.

The White Rhinoceros is the largest of the present-day rhinoceroses though it is not so tall as the Indian Rhinoceros. A large male may weigh $3\frac{1}{2}$ tonnes. The skin is pale grey and is almost hairless.

White Rhinoceros charging

It is certainly much paler than the Black Rhinoceros but the English name "White" is probably a corruption of the Dutch word "wijd" meaning "wide". This refers to the shape of the lips which are not pointed but broad and rather square-shaped (this animal is often called the Square-lipped Rhinoceros). White Rhinoceroses are grazers, not browsers, and the upper lip works very much like the sail of a reaping machine, folding grass into the mouth so that it can be plucked. These rhinoceroses live in herds of about a dozen animals. The males tend to set up local territories which they mark with piles of dung, while the females wander from territory to territory.

White Rhinoceros

Indian Rhinoceros with baby

When female rhinoceroses come into heat the male mounts from behind and takes from twenty minutes to one hour to transfer his sperm so that an egg can be fertilized. It takes fifteen to seventeen months before the baby is born. The baby has no horns and weighs one-fortieth the weight of its mother. It takes three or four years to be fully grown and may live for twenty-five years or even longer.

Rhinoceroses move by walking, trotting and cantering, but they are unable to gallop like horses.

6

Perissodactyls of the past

Today the seventeen species in the three families of horses, tapirs and rhinoceroses are all that is left of a much larger group of related animals. We know of many extinct members of these families and the fossil record of the horses is so complete that it is possible to trace step by step the changes from the little *Hyracotherium* (sometimes called *Eohippus*) to the horses of today. There were also several other families of animals in this Order which have now completely died out. Though it is very hard to be sure of the exact shape and colour, it has been possible to work out what sort of animals they were and why they died out.

Fifty million years ago in the period known as the Eocene, an animal called *Hyracotherium*, with three or four toes on each foot and about the size of a hare, lived in North America. It is from *Hyracotherium* that the horses developed. It lived on the leaves of bushes growing in forests and swamps. As the years went by its descendants began to eat grass and live in open plains. Their teeth got much longer, enabling the animals to chew the very abrasive grass leaves, the number of toes was reduced, the legs became straighter and the brain became bigger.

Mesohippus which lived thirty million years ago

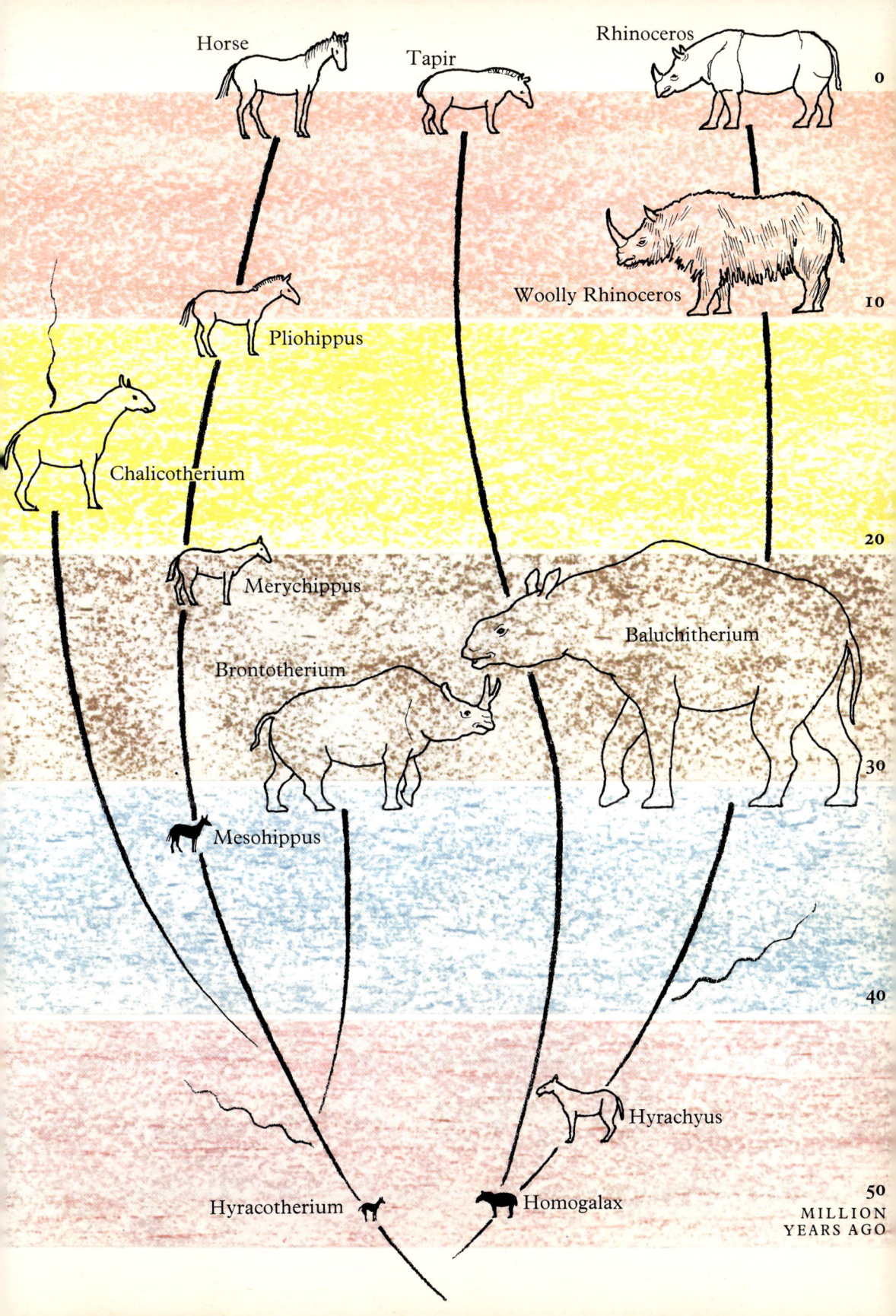

Horse

Tapir

Rhinoceros

0

Woolly Rhinoceros

10

Pliohippus

Chalicotherium

20

Merychippus

Baluchitherium

Brontotherium

30

Mesohippus

40

Hyrachyus

Hyracotherium

Homogalax

50
MILLION
YEARS AGO

had only three toes on each foot. *Merychippus* lived twenty million years ago and still had three toes on each foot but its teeth were much longer. It was about the size of a donkey. *Pliohippus* lived ten million years ago and was the size of a pony. It only had one toe on each foot but some of the bones of the other two toes were still present. Finally, the modern horses appeared in the last five million years. The bones of the other two toes on each foot appear only as little splints fused on to the main bone of the remaining toe.

During the history of animal evolution there have been many groups which have died out without leaving any descendants. The Brontotheres (also often called Titanotheres) lived about thirty million years ago and some were the size of an elephant but with enormous Y-shaped horn on the nose. They probably lived in forests and ate the leaves of trees which they may have pushed down with these horns. The Chalicotheres were another "blind alley" although they lived for about thirty-five million years until they finally died out only two million years ago. They were the size of horses but had three toes on each leg and each toe had two claws, not hoofs as in the other animals in the group. These claws were probably used to pull down and hold branches so that the Chalicotheres could eat the leaves.

Meanwhile the tapirs and rhinoceroses were

42

evolving from much smaller ancestors. The tapirs are descended from *Homogalax*. There has not been very much change except that the nose has got more and more flexible. Rhinoceroses began with *Hyrachyus* which lived about forty million years ago. The first true rhinoceroses, with horns made of compacted hair, lived thirty-five million years ago. One group, the Baluchitheres, lived in the forests of Southern Asia, where there are now deserts, and grew to stand at $5\frac{1}{2}$ metres at the shoulder, or about as high as the tallest giraffe. These animals must have weighed over fifteen tonnes and were the largest land mammals known. In the ice ages in Europe and Asia there lived a very hairy rhinoceros, the Woolly Rhinoceros, whose coat helped to keep out the intense cold.

Nowadays there are only five kinds of rhinoceros, but in the past a great many more lived in Africa, Europe and North America.

7

The future

The living horses, tapirs and rhinoceroses are the result of many millions of years of change, during most of which man was not around. Man has evolved much more quickly. In his present form he has only been on the earth for the last two million years or so and for most of this short time has made very little change on the world in which he lives. It was not until civilization began about ten thousand years ago that man began seriously to alter the ground surface and make it more and more difficult for some species to live. It was not until much more recently that man had the gun and the tractor and could destroy whole herds, and the land where they lived, in a few months or years. So what has happened is that the pressure of all the things which make it difficult for a species of animals to survive has suddenly become much greater. If the next hundred years are like the last hundred years these animals will not survive.

Fortunately, man is not only able to do things to the earth's surface but he is also able to study the effects of what he has done, and to work out how he can stop some of the consequences. This is what we call "conservation". There are two important aspects to conservation. We can save some of the

44

Saved from extinction, Przewalski's Wild Horse

natural habitat of the species so that it can go on living and reproducing itself in the wild; and we can protect some of the members of the species in zoos and wildlife parks so that they can go on breeding whether or not the natural habitat still exists.

Of the seventeen species of horses, tapirs and rhinoceroses, two, the domestic Horse and the Donkey, are safe from extinction for a long time because they are now domestic animals. Grevy's Zebra, the Common Zebra, the Malayan Tapir, the Brazilian Tapir, Baird's Tapir and the Black Rhinoceros are still safe because their habitats are not yet seriously threatened though they all could be eliminated by indiscriminate hunting just as the Quagga was hunted to extinction a hundred years ago. Three species, the White Rhinoceros, the

Indian Rhinoceros and the Mountain Zebra, are safe in the wild only as long as the slender remnants of their habitats can be protected. The last of the Tarpans probably disappeared because none of its habitat was saved. The Onager, the Kiang and the Mountain Tapir live in places which cannot be easily protected and must be bred in zoos and parks if they are to survive. The Javan and the Sumatran Rhinoceroses are so near to extinction that they will be saved only with the greatest luck. Finally, Przewalski's Horse is probably already extinct in the wild and only lives in zoological parks where it breeds without too much difficulty though the numbers are small.

Thus this small group of animals which we take so much for granted—imagine a world with no rhinoceroses!—are all in need of our active help if they are to survive and make the world a richer place for our own species to live in.

Index